ELIZABETH LEGAULT

Golden Retriever Puppy Handbook
Essential Guide for New and Soon-to-be Puppy Owners

Copyright © 2022 by Elizabeth Legault

All rights reserved. No part of this publication may be reproduced, stored or transmitted in any form or by any means, electronic, mechanical, photocopying, recording, scanning, or otherwise without written permission from the publisher. It is illegal to copy this book, post it to a website, or distribute it by any other means without permission.

First edition

This book was professionally typeset on Reedsy. Find out more at reedsy.com

Contents

1	Introduction	1
2	Chapter 1: Finding and Picking the Right Puppy	6
3	Chapter 2: What You Should Know Before You Get the Puppy	14
4	Chapter 3: How to Prepare Before Your Puppy Arrives	18
5	Chapter 4: When the Puppy Arrives Home	29
6	Conclusion	44
7	Resources	45

1

Introduction

Welcome to the Golden Retriever Puppy Handbook! My name is Elizabeth Legault, and I'm extremely excited to be writing this book! I decided to write this book because a friend of mine recently went through the experience of buying a Golden Retriever puppy. She spent countless hours researching the topics I will go over in this book in addition to asking questions about my experience raising my Golden puppies. I'll probably print out 20 copies and donate them to Goldenridge Kennels in Hampden, ME, owned by Roxanne and Leslie Ellsworth, so they can share them with their new and soon-to-be owners. This is the kennel where I bought all of my puppies. The puppies I have received from them have never had any issues. I owe the world to them for breeding the puppies that have brought so much love and happiness to my family.

The other reason I'm so excited to write this is because being an owner of Golden Retrievers has given me so much happiness and joy, and when I see others planning to get one, I want them to enjoy this experience as much as I did. Hopefully this book can ease people's minds and answer all of the questions most people have when interested in getting a puppy. Here is my attempt to do that.

A brief background about me.... I decided to get a Golden because my aunt had one, and everytime we went to visit her, my brother and I got to experience a dog who was gentle, kind, loveable and so sweet to be around. I remember thinking that when I got old enough to have my own dog, I would buy this breed first. In 2008, I got my first Golden Retriever, and we named her Auburn. She was my first born, my love, my world.

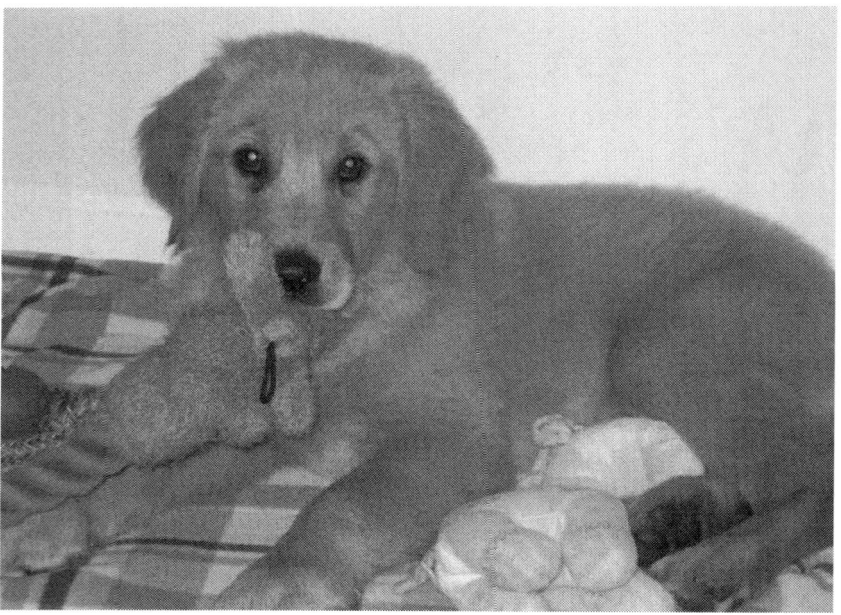

The name fit her well because she was an auburn color, but we really

INTRODUCTION

named her after Auburn University because my former father-in-law loved their football team. I didn't have kids yet, so I thought it would be a good experience to do a trial run with a dog. Boy, was I in for a surprise! I never knew there was so much to know about owning a puppy. We lost Auburn last year at the age of 13. She led an amazing life, and she will always be remembered in our hearts. We currently have a new puppy in our lives (Mango) and two other Goldens that are 3 (Willow) and 5 (Orabella, Bella for short) years old.

Bella is the British Golden, and Willow is the American Golden in the picture below.

This book is not one that will give you every little detail there is to know about Golden Retrievers in general. I'm simply here to deliver the most important details that I feel people should know before they take the

INTRODUCTION

time to research a breeder, purchase a puppy, and then bring the puppy home, without needing to flip through hundreds of pages to find what you are really looking for.

If you have been contemplating getting a Golden Retriever, I am here to share with you that it will be the best decision you make! Especially if you have young children, this is the puppy for you!

With all those things said, it's time to jump in and get started!

2

Chapter 1: Finding and Picking the Right Puppy

Researching Breeders

I think this was the hardest part about getting a puppy. How do you research and find the best breeder out there?

First point I want to share, you have to be very careful nowadays with people scamming you on the internet. I do not recommend talking to any individual who reaches out to you if you post you are looking for a puppy or anyone that does not have an extensive website for you to view. I thought I would touch on some Facebook Marketbook red flags to be aware of:

- Lowered price Golden Retriever (Most Goldens from reputable breeders will cost $1500-$3500)
- A profile that was created recently

CHAPTER 1: FINDING AND PICKING THE RIGHT PUPPY

- A seller that asks to meet you somewhere or your house. (Most breeders have you come to their home to pick up the puppy.)
- If you can't see the puppy before purchasing it, don't buy it. (All breeders will have you pick out your puppy from a litter according to the order in which you put your deposit down. Since COVID happened, some breeders are allowing buyers to pick their puppy over Zoom, which has been a common experience I have found recently. Don't be nervous about this, but be cautious.
- If the seller directs you to another site to communicate, it's a scam.
- Google the kennel or the owner's name to see if scam alerts pop up. Usually you are not the first person to be scammed, so there should be something that pops up if it is suspicious.

Now let's focus on how to find specific breeders in your area. I find that the best method is to ask your local veterinarian, the one you will be using, who they recommend. They have experience with meeting puppies, and they usually know or can find breeders that are around your area. In addition, feel free to ask a trusted friend who has one. You will find that you know at least one person that has a Golden Retriever now or has owned one in the past. There are three places that I will recommend from my friends who own Goldens today.

- Goldenridge Kennels in Hampden, Maine (https://goldenridgekennels.com)
- Carolina Lakeside Goldens in Rockhill, SC (https://carolinalakesidegoldens.com)
- Blue Star Golden Retrievers in Kingston, MA https://www.facebook.com/Bluestargoldenretrievers

Another recommendation would be to go on the AKC (American Kennel

Club) website (www.akg.org) and click on "Find a puppy" at the top. The thing I like about the AKC is that it is the only purebred registry in the US that does investigations and inspections of the kennel to ensure that it is in compliance with the standards of the safety and welfare of their dogs and the environment that they are living in.

Please take note that if your puppy comes with AKC papers, this does not mean that your puppy will be healthy and have no problems in the future. You can never guarantee that your puppy won't experience health issues when you buy from a breeder. Unfortunately it is the risk you will need to take. There are "puppy lemon laws" that are different in each state, so be aware that you can look into getting a refund if your Golden is discovered to be unhealthy within a given period of time. In addition, make sure to read the contract you sign that the owner gives to you with your puppy. I always recommend seeing your veterinarian right when you bring the puppy home. Please refer to the section in Chapter 4, called *Finding and Visiting the Vet* for a helpful suggestion.

Questions to Ask the Breeders

As you are researching to find the best breeder out there, it is important to call them directly to ask them specific questions. What questions should you ask? I have selected the Top 10 questions that I find have been important when getting a puppy. I created this list to make sure that you find the best breeder and puppy for you!

1. Make sure that you ask to meet the parents. Seeing the parents temperament will help you to see what your puppy will be like.
2. Ask how the parents' health has been. Any genetic diseases?
3. Ask how long they have been breeding Goldens? Ask any questions

CHAPTER 1: FINDING AND PICKING THE RIGHT PUPPY

about the breed. If they are knowledgeable about the breed, that is a good sign.
4. Ask how they socialize their dogs and their puppies when they are born. It is best that they are around other dogs, children, people and even other animals, like cats. I have three cats that live in my house so that was one of my biggest concerns. See how well our new puppy is adjusting to our family in the *Socialization* section under Chapter 4.
5. Ask what vaccinations the parents have and what vaccinations will the puppies get before coming home?
6. As we touched upon earlier, find out clearly from the breeder what their refund policy is in regards to a health condition that is discovered during the initial check or if they will reclaim the puppy if you decide you can no longer take care of the puppy.
7. When can you take the puppy home?
8. What number pick are you? Will you get to select the puppy and what week?
9. Where can we contact you after taking the puppy home?
10. Do you have references?

Answers will definitely vary when speaking with different breeders, but after hearing the answers to these questions, you should be able to get a sense of which breeder you like the most and from whom you want to get your puppy. The waiting list and distance to the kennel from your home are other factors that you need to keep in consideration.

Picking the Right Puppy

How do you choose the right puppy for your family? When you see them all together and you go to pick one out, all you can think about is,

"How do I just select one?"

This was our experience a few months ago. In the picture above is Mango and her brothers and sisters. They pretty much look the same, and ALL of them are adorable! So which one do you pick?

After selecting your breeder, you need to know which kind of Golden Retriever you want. There are three kinds; American, Canadian and British Golden Retrievers. The only difference between the American and Canadian Golden Retriever is their coat. The Canadian has a longer coat than the American breed, but they both vary in color from being

CHAPTER 1: FINDING AND PICKING THE RIGHT PUPPY

very light to darker in color. The British Golden Retriever is usually white. As you saw in my introduction, I have an American and a British Golden Retriever. There is a big difference between the two colorwise. Everyone always asks if my British Golden is a lab. Not a lot of people know about this type of Golden and are shocked to hear that she is one. I love the color of my British Golden because she is so unique! Just remember not to wear black when you want to take this type of puppy to the vet!

After you know which type of Golden you want and you have put your deposit down for a puppy, your next step will be to select your puppy from the litter in the order that you put your deposit down. Your breeder will inform you of this when you put your deposit down. I have been first and second-to-last in order for my puppies. It doesn't matter where you are in the order, unless you are last, and you don't get a choice. If that happens and you want to wait, ask the breeder if you can be first in the next litter. It is exciting to know that you are going to have the opportunity to pick one that you hope is going to be the best puppy of the litter!

Before you select, you need to think about what you want from your Golden Retriever. Think about the following:

- Male or Female
- Size
- Type of Golden
- Style (athletic, blockhead)
- Color
- Personality: I always pick the calm ones. I never pick a puppy who is wild, never stops and looks out of control. I love the puppies who come and want to sit in my lap. This is up to you and what you

desire the most!

Talk to the breeder about what you are looking for, and they can give you suggestions on which puppy will be the best fit for you. They are with the puppies the most and can tell you what each puppy's temperament is like. Carolina Lakeside Goldens that I mentioned above share the temperament of each puppy on their website as do some of the other breeders I have researched. Feel free to ask the breeder too.

Here are some helpful tips to help you decide:

- Observe the puppies interacting with each other. Who is submissive and who is dominant?
- Who is the runt of the litter?
- Look at the energy level. (As I explained above, I usually go for the calm and quiet ones.)
- Look at how the puppies are interacting with people. I always bring my kids with me to select our puppy to see which puppy goes best with their personalities. Look to see if the dog is fearful, outgoing, a chewer etc. Take notes if you need to when you are there.
- Pick them up and cradle them. If the puppy squirms, it could possibly mean that it is more dominant than a puppy who relaxes in your arms. I would consider that a submissive puppy.
- Touch the puppy's paw, tail, ears, belly, and mouth. Make sure that none of these actions cause a concerning reaction from the puppy.
- Toss a toy or your keys to see how alert the puppy is.
- Make sure that you pick a healthy puppy too. Eyes should be clear, nose should not be runny. Make sure that they are fluffy and soft, that they are not skinny and have some meat on them, and that they have the puppy bounce.

CHAPTER 1: FINDING AND PICKING THE RIGHT PUPPY

Just remember that sometimes a puppy will find you and this checklist will go out the window!

3

Chapter 2: What You Should Know Before You Get the Puppy

Time Commitment

All puppies are a huge time commitment, but especially a Golden Retriever because they are devoted and loving to you. They crave attention and love from their owners. In return they will give you the same so this is why the breed is worth the time and energy you will put into them.

You will need to make time to throw the ball to them, take them for a walk in the park or around your neighborhood. Of course all puppies crave attention, but Goldens are known to want to be around their owners all of the time. If you leave them alone for long periods of time, they can be destructive if they don't get the attention and exercise needed each day. As they get older, they aren't as needy.

Here are some other things you should know in regards to time commitment:

CHAPTER 2: WHAT YOU SHOULD KNOW BEFORE YOU GET THE PUPPY

- Make sure you exercise your puppy about 1 ½ - 2 hours a day. Puppy day care is a great option, but make sure that you do some research and read reviews before dropping them off.
- Make sure that you are taking your puppy outside every ½ hour or before. I will talk more about this in Chapter 4 under *Putting the Training to Work*.
- Goldens have a beautiful coat that needs to be brushed. This will take up to a few hours each week.
- Training a puppy takes time too. You can start working with them at home before taking them to puppy school. There are so many YouTube videos that teach you tricks on how to teach them to sit, lie down and paw. It's never too early to start working with them. Mango has mastered all of the skills mentioned above. They are really smart puppies and pick up training really fast, but you need to consistently work with them. It only takes about 15 minutes a day.
- In the beginning when they first come home, they have very small bladders. Expect to wake up several times during the night to bring them out. Bring them outside, without talking to them, and put them back into the crate. I will explain why this is important in the next section, *Crate/House training*.

Remember that Golden Retriever puppies are like babies, and they can change your entire life, routine, and schedule, but they are definitely worth it!

Cost of Owning a Puppy

With everything else in life, a puppy costs money. I wanted to list some of the expenses associated with getting a puppy. I am only going to go over the puppy costs. When the puppy turns one, there are additional costs that will be required of you each year to maintain their shots, food, dog toys, beds, heartworm, flea and tick, leashes, collars, and emergency vet bills for sicknesses or if your dog gets hurt. These are expenses for any puppy, not just for a Golden.

Let's list the most important things needed (minimum):

- The puppy: $1500-3500
- Crate (this is only if you are going to be doing crate training). I would advise you to crate train your puppies. It is not a punishment to do this. Puppies enjoy their crates, and sometimes you will find them going in the crate on their own if you leave the door open. I will talk more about crates in the *Crate/House Training* section in this chapter. $40-$100
- Toys: $10-$30 a month
- Food: $50-$70 every 6 -10 weeks
- Collars/leash/harness: $30-$100
- Dog bowls for water and food: $30-$50
- Gates if needed to block a section off in your home: $50-$100
- Poop bags: $5-$10
- Dog bed: $30-$100
- Puppy's first visit to the vet: $75-100
- Snuggle puppy (not required, but recommended): $20-$40
- Storage container to store the food: $20-$50
- Training treats (you can use hotdogs for another option): $10-$20
- Puppy brush, puppy shampoo, cotton balls to clean ears, nail clippers, toothbrush & toothpaste: $50-$100
- Spayed or Neutered: $75- $800 (You can look at your local MSPCA.

CHAPTER 2: WHAT YOU SHOULD KNOW BEFORE YOU GET THE PUPPY

They offer low costs to get this done.)
- Petco offers $15 to cut your puppy's toenails and to get a bath. You can bring them as many times as you like until they are six months old. Gets them used to going so they don't have anxiety when they are older. ***Shout out to Plaistow, NH Petco Grooming who takes care of my Goldens. The staff there is amazing, especially Vanessa!

Most of the items you can find cheap at Marshalls, TJ Maxx, Amazon. Keep your eye out for deals at Petco, Pet Smart, and Chewy. I just signed up for Vital care at Petco, which is definitely worth the money! You get deals on your food, grooming, and you get reward money each month to spend on whatever you like. Contact Petco to find more out about this.

4

Chapter 3: How to Prepare Before Your Puppy Arrives

Type of Food You Should Get

Before your puppy comes home, you should purchase the puppy food that the breeder has had them on for the past 3-5 weeks. Do not buy a large bag unless you plan to keep them on this food until they turn one. You don't want to start them on a brand new food when they come home. This could lead to an upset stomach and digestive issues. Trust me when I say that changing their diet can lead to diarrhea, which leads to you getting up multiple times during the night. Not fun and very tiring for both you and the puppy!

Do you have to keep them on this certain food? No! I like to keep my puppies on the breeders food for about a month, unless I see that the food does not work with them. Make sure that you ask your veterinarian which food they suggest and then gradually wean them onto their new food. Every veterinarian is different. We use the Purina Puppy Pro Plan which was recommended by our vet.

CHAPTER 3: HOW TO PREPARE BEFORE YOUR PUPPY ARRIVES

This process of switching foods should take about 5-7 days. Here is the schedule you should follow:

- Day 1-3, mix a greater percentage of old food than the new food. I usually do 2/3 of old food and 1/3 of the new food. We will talk more about how much total to feed your puppy in Chapter 4: *How Much Food to Feed Your Puppy*.
- Day 4-5, mix half and half–¼ cup of each.
- Day 6-7, mix a greater percentage of the new food than the old food, 2/3 of the new food and 1/3 of the old food
- By Day 8, you should be able to give 100% of the new food. ½ cup per serving.

It is important to monitor your puppy, watching how their stool samples are. If you see that your puppy is constantly having loose stools, vomiting or not eating at all, contact your veterinarian for suggestions.

Benefits of Toys and Which Ones Are Great to Buy

Toys are a necessity for puppies and even dogs, and they are well worth the money you invest in them. Toys are important for many reasons, and I will quickly share with you the benefits of getting them:

- Distracts your dog from getting bored and keeps them out of trouble.
- Certain toys can provide comfort not only for anxiety, but for their teeth. Puppies, like babies, need teething toys to help soothe the pain.
- You can use them to exercise your puppy.
- Corrects behavioral issues that might include digging, chewing,

biting, etc.
- Certain toys can help keep your puppy's teeth clean.
- Great for training and stimulating their minds.
- Important to your puppy's development

Now that we can see that puppies can't live without toys, let me share with you my Goldens' favorites. There are so many toys out there, and trust me when I say we have tried many of them! I would consider these to be the Top 10 Best Toys for Golden Retrievers.

1. **Snuggle Puppy**-When you take your puppy home the first night, remember that the puppy is leaving his/her mom and dad for the first time. This can cause anxiety and stress and cause your puppy to whine and bark in their crate at night. The Snuggle puppy is a calming aid that helps with crate training. It comes with a heat pack and a real pulsing heartbeat to mimic being with the puppy's parents. You can find this product on Amazon.
2. Teething toys-As we discussed above, it is critical to purchase teething toys to help ease the pain of teething. **Nylabone** offers some great toys that help to massage their gums. I usually purchase the **Nylabone Teething Pacifier Puppy Chew Toy, Nylabone Teething Rings Puppy Chew Toy, or the Nylabone Puppy Triple Pack.**
3. I also enjoy the **Kong Puppy Products** because you can fill the toy with a treat that they have to nibble on to get to or you can freeze them.
4. Investing in a durable chew toy will be a smart decision to keep your Golden from any destructive chewing. **KONG Jump'N Jack Dog Toy** is our favorite. There are grooves on the toy to help

CHAPTER 3: HOW TO PREPARE BEFORE YOUR PUPPY ARRIVES

remove food debris and plaque. You can use this for chew sessions for a fun game of catch.

5. **Kong Wobbler Treat Dispensing Toy** provides entertainment for hours and keeps your Golden puppy constantly busy. When your puppy touches this toy with its paw and moves the toy around, a treat will dispense for the puppy to eat. This toy can also be used to slow down their mealtime, which helps with their weight management.
6. **Tikaton Indestructible Chew Toy** comes in three flavors (bacon, beef and peanut butter). They are built to last for many hours of playtime. They come in three different sizes so pick the small one for your puppy. As they grow, you can purchase the medium one and eventually the large size.
7. Golden Retrievers love to "retrieve". The **ChuckIt Classic Launcher** is a terrific way to exercise your dog without wearing you out. It comes with a tennis ball and launcher. Great training toy to get your dogs to retrieve the ball and bring it back to you.
8. If you want to play tug a war with your Golden or play a game of fetch, the **Mammoth 3 Knot Dog Rope Toy** is a great value because of its versatility and what it has to offer. My only suggestion with this toy is not to leave it around. It is not a durable toy and can not withstand a puppy constantly chewing on it. You want to make sure that they don't ingest any pieces of the rope.
9. Toys that squeak are cute in the beginning when a puppy hears it squeak for the first time, but can be annoying after a short period of time. If you wanted to get a squeaky toy, the **Frisco Flat Plush Squeaking Duck Dog Toy** is my favorite. This toy is stuffing free so there will be less mess if your puppy destroys it. As your puppy gets older, you will find that you don't want to spend money on toys that are stuffed, because they will be destroyed within the hour, and you just wasted anywhere from $10-$15. My puppy

likes to carry this toy around in her mouth all day, and it can be used for fetch.

Kong Jumbler Football Dog Toy is for the Golden who is all about ball toys. There are two balls in this one toy (a tennis ball trapped inside a football shaped toy) Our puppy loves to use this to play tug of war with our older dogs.

Crate/ What You Need For It

Setting up your crate before the puppy arrives is a must! You want to make sure that you start crate training the first day your puppy comes home. If you go back to Chapter 2: *Crate and House Training,* I explained what type of crate to buy and why it is important to have one. For this section let's discuss how to set up your dog's crate for comfort and safety. Remember that all puppies are different, and you need to make changes according to how your puppy is doing within your home.

- It's nice for your puppy to have some type of bed to lie on when they are in their crate. Some puppies like to snuggle and curl up in something warm while other puppies don't need any bedding at all. If you were to purchase a bed, make sure that it is washable, durable and waterproof, especially during the potty training days. My recommendation to meet all of the qualities is the **K9 Ballistics Tuff Crate Pad.** If your puppy chews through this within 120 days, the company will give you store credit to purchase another one. I wouldn't suggest that you put a blanket in your crate. If puppies get bored in the crate, they might start to chew on this. If she/he ends up swallowing the pieces, it could lead to an internal blockage and

CHAPTER 3: HOW TO PREPARE BEFORE YOUR PUPPY ARRIVES

you will end up in the emergency room.

- Goldens should have access to water at all times, and as long as it is not affecting the puppy's potty training, feel free to purchase "clip on" water bowls or a water bottle that attaches to the crate. Two suggestions would be to use the **Midwest Snap'y Fit Stainless Steel Bowl** or the **Choco Nose No-Drip Dog Water Bottle**. My puppies used the water bottle because it was attached to the outside of the crate and you didn't have to worry about them chewing on it or destroying it. Some puppies have trouble understanding the concept of a lickable water bottle at first. Tip: put peanut butter on the nozzle where the water comes out, and they will figure it out soon enough. I would not suggest putting a bowl of water on the floor in the crate. Goldens love to play in water, and this can lead to quite a mess!
- Do not put their food in the crate for two reasons:

1. They might step on the bowl, and the food will go everywhere
2. You don't want the bowl to become their new chew toy when bored in the crate

- "Crate toys" can remain in your puppy's crate. You know your puppy the best so make sure to pick safe and durable toys that don't need supervision. There should be at least one good chew toy in there that your puppy loves. I find that leaving the "crate toys" in their safe space makes it exciting for the puppy when she/he goes back in the crate. We can relate this concept to a toddler. If your toddler is constantly seeing the same toys and you pull out a new one, think about how excited they are to see something new. Same

goes for a puppy!
- We can't forget the Snuggle puppy! If you start to see that your puppy is chewing on and starting to rip the Snuggle puppy, only put it in at night when the puppy is exhausted from playing all day, and they know it is time to sleep.
- Take your puppy's collar off while in the crate. This is because the collar can get caught on the crate bars and can lead to strangulation. It doesn't happen often but let's try to avoid any potentially hazardous situation. They do have breakaway-type safety collars and ID tags that will lay flat on the collar if you want to feel more comfortable that your dog will be safe at all times. You should be monitoring your puppy at all times so in reality this is not a necessity.

At the end of the day, your puppy only needs a few major items in the crate to create a cozy, friendly place where your dog will enjoy spending time.

Other essentials needed

"I'm getting a new puppy, what do I need? Do you have a puppy checklist?" This is a common question that new and soon-to-be owners ask the breeders when purchasing their first puppy. I thought I would provide this checklist to save you from asking and to ease your anxiety. You can refer to Chapter 2: *Cost of Having a Puppy* if you want to get a ballpark figure on how much it will cost you.

Here is the checklist of other essential items needed:

- Water and food bowls

CHAPTER 3: HOW TO PREPARE BEFORE YOUR PUPPY ARRIVES

- Leash, collar, harness, pet tag
- Toys and chew toys
- Grannicks Bitter Apple spray to help deter a puppy from biting or apple cider vinegar/water mix
- Stain and odor remover
- Training treats or you can use hotdogs.
- Dog brush
- Puppy shampoo
- Poop bags
- Gate if needed
- Nail trimmer
- Toothbrush and paste
- Flea and tick meds (Talk to your vet first to see when to start your first application)
- Heartworm meds (Talk to your vet first to see when to start your first application)
- Food container

Checklist of items already discussed:

- Crate
- Bed for the crate
- Clip on water bowl or bottle
- Puppy food
- Puppy toys
- Chewing toys
- Snuggle puppy

If you count ALL of the essential items, you have about 30 items needed to buy, which can be pretty pricey. You have 8-10 weeks to wait (depending on the breeder) so spread out the costs by buying 4 items per week. Remember to look in the stores mentioned in Chapter 2: *Cost of Owning a Puppy* to help save you some money!

Finding the Vet

If you already have a veterinarian, you can skip this section. Make sure that you find your veterinarian before you bring home the puppy. You can either ask friends and family for referrals, or you can use Google to search for vets in your area. It is important that you read the reviews and pick the vet that matches what you are looking for. Once you select the veterinarian, make an advanced appointment for a few days after you get the puppy. Have your new veterinarian look over the puppy and do a health check. You want to do this to ensure that the puppy looks happy and healthy. In addition, you want your vet to keep your puppy healthy from that moment on.

If the veterinarian sees that your puppy has medical issues, you can choose to either get treatment for the puppy right away before their condition becomes worse or speak to the breeder about the refund policy or possible help with the vet bills.

How to Prepare the Inside/Outside of Your Home

CHAPTER 3: HOW TO PREPARE BEFORE YOUR PUPPY ARRIVES

Preparing to bring a puppy home is very similar to babyproofing your house when your toddler is learning how to crawl around. A new pup, like a toddler, will tend to get into anything and everything and put it in its mouth.

Here is a puppy-proofing checklist on how you can "puppy-proof" your house and what to watch out for when you take your puppy outside.

Inside of the home:

- Put away anything a puppy can pick up or get into. Examples: shoes, house plants, decorations, clothing
- Remove anything that hangs that they can pull down.
- Lock up cabinets and make sure there are no hazardous materials around.
- If you have young children, make sure that their toys are put away.
- Pick up any cords and make sure wires are in a secure location.
- Get the gates set up to secure your puppy in a confined space. I have a gate at the bottom of the stairs and one that leads into my dining room. The puppy has access to anything in the living room/kitchen.
- Roll up your carpets until your puppy is potty trained. Puppies love to go to the bathroom on an area rug. Why do you ask? Very simple....Breeders might train the puppies to go on a pee pad. When the puppy sees a rectangular shape rug similar to a pee pad, they associate these two things to be the same.
- Make sure that toilet seats are down. Puppies like to drink toilet water, and they can easily drown in it.
- Keep all sharp objects away.
- Pick up any small items that can be choking hazards.

Outside of the Home:

- Make sure that your puppy cannot access the garbage cans.
- Move any pesticides into a safe area.
- Fence in the yard with a fence high enough to prevent the puppy from jumping over it or put in an invisible fence. Everyone has different opinions about the Invisible Fence. My Goldens were easily trained on this, and it has worked wonders for our family.
- Pick up after your dogs so the puppy won't eat other feces and even their own.
- Just make sure that you supervise your puppy when you let them out. It is important that they don't put anything in their mouths, like rocks and other small objects.
- Be aware of predators and other potential hazards.

Puppies, like babies, are dependent on you to keep them safe. It is a huge responsibility to take care of a puppy, but it is worth it in the end!

5

Chapter 4: When the Puppy Arrives Home

Yay! The time has finally come to pick up your puppy from the breeder! By now, you should have everything purchased and set up to make this a smooth transition when bringing your puppy home! There are many different situations that will happen when your puppy arrives home. I thought I would share my experiences, and hopefully it is similar to yours!

Introducing Your Puppy to Your Other Dogs/Animals

Every time I brought a new puppy home, I had to remember that there were other animals in the house. I have always had Goldens so I have to say that this was always an easy transition, as I'm sure it will be for you too. Golden Retrievers are very accepting of a puppy of their own kind, especially if they are on the younger side themselves. If you need more help with the transition, then feel free to ask an expert or use Google. I am definitely not an expert, but I am open to share with you what worked best for us in our story below.

We just welcomed Mango into the house in June 2022. At that time, Willow and Bella were 3 and 5 years old. For the initial meeting my friend, Monica, paid close attention to Mango while I focused and gave attention to Willow and Bella. It is important to make sure that each dog/puppy is on a leash. I always have them meet in the yard because my Goldens aren't really territorial in our yard. If you have a territorial dog, I would suggest that you meet in another place first, like a park or another open area. You can expect the dogs to sniff each other, then they will circle around each other, and possibly playtime might happen. Some older dogs might ignore the puppy. Bella was that way! It doesn't mean that she doesn't like Mango, she would rather just meet another human than a puppy. She is the type of dog that you take to the dog park and instead of "meeting and greeting" other dogs, she will "meet and greet" their owners instead. Bella should have been a service animal dog because she loves people!

If the animals fight, gently pull them away with the leash and guide them further away with a treat. After they meet, try going for a walk together. If the walk is successful, then you can bring the puppy home and try out the same process in the house.

If the process wasn't successful, my suggestion would be to keep them apart until they adjust. The older the dog is, the harder this transition can be because older dogs are set in their ways. Auburn was 8 year old when we brought Bella into the house. She was not happy with Bella at first, biting her tail and her ankles. She would growl and snap at Bella, but her tail was always wagging so you knew that she was not going to attack. Auburn just wanted Bella to know that she was old, and she would play with her on her own time. They eventually became best friends until Willow came into the house two years later! I have found that the new puppy always plays with the one that is closer in age!

CHAPTER 4: WHEN THE PUPPY ARRIVES HOME

I thought it would be fun to show you how Mango has adjusted to our animals.

Pepper, our cat, came down and started bathing Mango and then fell asleep on her.

CHAPTER 4: WHEN THE PUPPY ARRIVES HOME

Mango and Willow playing tug of war together. Bella usually sits and watches them play.

Introducing Your Puppy to Your Children

Your children and your new puppy have a lot in common. They are both impatient, excitable, and curious. When they first meet, it will be really important that you do all the right steps to ensure that it will be a successful encounter. Remember that first impressions are important. If you aren't cautious, your puppy could become fearful of your children, which could lead to an unhappy ending.

Here are some helpful steps for the first meeting:

1. Make sure that you are in the center of the room so a puppy doesn't feel cornered.

CHAPTER 4: WHEN THE PUPPY ARRIVES HOME

2. Have your children sit on the floor and let the puppy come to them. You should do this each time until your puppy is comfortable in your home and with your children.
3. Explain to your children that they need to be calm, keep their voices to a whisper, and no sudden movements.
4. Puppies look like cute teddy bears, so you need to teach your children to be gentle and not to squeeze them. Remind them that the puppy is a living creature that feels scared and nervous, just like they do.
5. If the puppy starts to nibble their hands or bite, have the child hand a chew toy to the puppy to remind them that their fingers/hands are not chew toys.

Never leave your puppy and child unattended, regardless of how easygoing your puppy is. Puppies can have their off days and for the safety of your child and your new puppy, please have them develop their relationship under supervision.

Visiting the Vet

Now that your puppy is home, it should be time to visit the veterinarian. You should already have an appointment booked for the vet to take a look at your puppy. Please refer to Chapter 3: *Finding the vet.*

You should always be prepared for your puppy's first visit to the vet. I am big on checklists, if you haven't noticed so far, so I thought I would create one for you to help you remember what to bring to the vet:

- A stool sample that is fresh. Try to get one in the morning before you go. Veterinarians will run some tests to make sure they don't see anything in their stool.

- Any questions or concerns you may have so far about your puppy.
- The paperwork from the breeder. This paperwork is important to the veterinarian so they can see the puppy's birth date, weight, if any shots were given etc.
- Paperwork that the veterinarian might have given you to fill out.
- Leash, collar or harness/leash
- Observation notes that you have taken in regards to your puppy. Appetite? Drinking a lot of water? What does their stool look like? Crate Training? How the puppy is getting along with the other animals? Or children?
- Chew toy in case the puppy gets bored and wants to bite.

Your veterinarian should take this visit to provide you with the information needed to raise a happy and healthy puppy. At times visiting the vet can be expensive, but it is well worth it in the end. You are basically paying money up front to prevent your puppy from serious health issues in the future.

Exercise Your Puppy

Golden Retrievers are considered high-energy dogs, so in order for them to stay mentally and physically healthy, we need to exercise them. We need to be careful not to over-exercise them too from when you bring them home until they are three months old. If you over-exercise your puppy, there could be bone and joint issues in the future. Puppies need time for their muscles to grow.

My veterinarian always taught me the five-minute rule. You only exercise them five minutes for each month that your puppy is alive. For example: one-month-old puppy–5 minutes, two-month-old puppy–10

CHAPTER 4: WHEN THE PUPPY ARRIVES HOME

minutes, etc. This can occur two times a day. You can break up the time by varying your activities. For example, Mango is three months old. We walk her for 10 minutes and then play fetch with her for 5 minutes. We try and switch it up each day. Sometimes when we don't have time for a walk, Willow exercises Mango by playing tug of war or just gently biting and chasing each other. I will never have just one dog again, because they do keep each other busy.

If you don't have another dog or you don't have the time to exercise your puppy, think about putting your puppy in doggy day care. The Puppy Day Care will exercise your puppy, but they will also kennel them so they can get rest time too. Puppy Day Care is used to help with Socialization, which we can talk about when we get to that section below.

Giving the exercise needed for your puppy is a very important aspect so they can live a happy and healthy life!

How Much Food to Feed Your Puppy

Golden Retrievers are known for their obesity, which can cause joint problems in their future so it is important not to overfeed your puppy. I like to check in with my veterinarian for advice on this topic, but I have found that my vet has said the same thing for all three puppies. Up until your puppy is six months old you should be feeding them three times a day. Here is the schedule:

- 2 months: ½ cup 3 times a day
- 3 months: ⅔ cup 3 times a day
- 4 months: ¾ cup 3 times a day
- 5-6 months: 1 cup 3 times a day

- 6-7 months: 1 ½ cup 2 times a day

Knowing the amount of food your Golden should eat after this can be tricky, but feel free to consult your veterinarian to see their thoughts. If they are overweight, they might switch your puppy to 1 cup or less 2 times a day.

Your Biting Puppy

It is extremely normal for play biting to occur when you are interacting with your puppy. Since the Golden has razor like teeth as a puppy, it can be a painful and not an enjoyable experience. It is possible to train away "play biting" with a few different ways. Let me share them with you:

- My favorite is called the "Ow" method in our household. When a puppy bites you, yell "Ow" in a very loud voice, cross your arms and storm off. When puppies bite their own mother or one of their littermates, they will yelp, warning them to stop. Giving your puppy a chew toy to substitute for your hand is another method that you can use to stop the bad behavior immediately.
- Some owners will use a bitter spray to spray objects they are biting or an apple cider vinegar/water mix to spray lightly at the puppy when they are biting.

If your puppy seems to be biting for aggression instead of play biting, make sure that you consult a trainer for further information on how to handle these negative behaviors.

CHAPTER 4: WHEN THE PUPPY ARRIVES HOME

Booking puppy training

Adding puppy school into your schedule is beneficial for both you and your puppy. Not only does it help your puppy socialize with other animals and people, it helps create a bond between you and your puppy. Here are six benefits to puppy training:

1. When you take your puppy to the vet, having a trained animal helps the veterinarian examine your pet more easily, which is less stressful on your puppy.
2. It is easier when you want to take your dog out into public to have a trained puppy.
3. Helps your puppy to be confident and friendly to other dogs and people.
4. Helps fix negative behaviors such as: biting, jumping, running away, etc.
5. Teaches your puppy not to ignore you.
6. Learn to communicate with your puppy so you can understand and grow together.

There are many trainers and training programs out there. You need to surf the internet to find out which ones are near you and if they come highly recommended. You need to read through the reviews and decide which trainer matches up with you and your puppy's needs.

Crate Training

Many people believe that crate training is considered punishment, but in reality it calms your dogs and relieves their anxiety. Having an enclosed space where your puppy feels comforted, safe and warm is important for the dog's development and also your sanity! All of my puppies were crate-trained until the age of two, and now I can leave them for hours without any issues.

How do you know which crate to pick?

I bought a travel crate for Willow that was made of fabric. I thought it was the best investment I could buy. It was a crate that was easy to fold and I could take it anywhere. One day I came home and found Willow waiting for me at the door. I couldn't understand why she wasn't in her crate. After further investigation, I noticed that she had chewed a hole in the fabric and squeezed through. It looked like she had spent hours creating this hole. Wire crates, I would suggest, are the best crates to buy. They not only provide the best ventilation, but they are extremely easy to clean. Plastic crates are good too, but the wire crates allows your Golden to be able to see out of the crate and know that their family is still around them.

Most puppies/dogs will not go to the bathroom in their crate where they sleep. If you buy too large of a crate, the puppy will sleep in one half of the crate and go to the bathroom in the other half. If you get a large crate, make sure you buy the one that comes with a divider to make the crate the right size for your puppy. Gradually move the divider to the back as your puppy grows. The best size for a Golden Retriever crate is 42".

One helpful tip that I remember our breeder told us when we brought Auburn home was to keep the crate in our bedroom at night and living room during the day. This way she could enjoy our company during the day and at night she would be close enough to us so we could hear her if she needed a potty break. It was also comforting for Auburn to

CHAPTER 4: WHEN THE PUPPY ARRIVES HOME

know that we were close by.

House Training

House training your Golden Retriever puppy can be very easy if you follow the tips below because they are very intelligent.

- Puppy pee pads are not necessary.
- Take your puppy outside 15 minutes after you feed them, immediately after waking up, and after playing with a toy, and as soon as you take the puppy out of the crate.
- Make a big deal when they go to the bathroom outside by praising them.
- Use the Noah Strategy: **N**-Never an **O**- Opportunity for an **A**- Accident to **H**- Happen
- When you take them outside, it is not playtime. If they start to play, they will forget that they have to go to the bathroom. When you bring them back in, they will then go to the bathroom. At night, it is important to remember not to talk to your puppy when they wake you up in the middle of the night. Take them out, let them go to the bathroom, and then bring them right back to their crate. If you start to talk to them, they might wake you up every night just for the attention that you gave them the night before.
- Do not leave them unattended. If you can't watch your puppy, put them in the crate, and then bring them immediately outside when you let them out.
- If you catch them about to go in the house, startle them in a nice way and say, "not in here" or "outside". Then praise them when they finish outside.
- Look for the signs that your puppy has to go: circling, sitting by the door, sniffing the ground more than normal and whining.

If you follow the steps in this guide carefully, your puppy will be going outside in no time!

Keeping your puppy in the crate/how long

If you have never crate-trained before, you might be curious about how long you can keep your puppy in a crate. We need to remember that puppies have a very small bladder and cannot be left in a crate for long periods of time. The suggested crate time is 1 hour for each month they are alive. Mango is three months old right now, so we do not put her in her crate for more than three hours. We put her in the crate when we need to run an errand or work for a couple of hours.

As you get to know your puppy, you will learn how long you can leave your puppy in the crate. Remember that you don't want to be stuck in one room for a long period of time in your home and neither does a puppy!

Socialization

Socializing your Golden with other animals/people will create not only a happy puppy, but a happy owner. A dog that is not socialized will be scared of new experiences and it will become more of a challenge to convince them that the experiences are fun the older that they get.

When Bella and Auburn were puppies they were socialized with other dogs during Puppy school, and they were brought to the Puppy park on a weekly basis. When Willow was a puppy, I did all of my training at home, since I had learned the skills necessary to teach her. I didn't get to take her to the Puppy park that often because of time restraints. Boy, did I make a mistake! Willow was scared of her own shadow. When I

CHAPTER 4: WHEN THE PUPPY ARRIVES HOME

took her for walks, she was skittish about objects that were around her like garbage barrels or blow-up Christmas ornaments. She was fearful when it came time to go into Petco to get groomed and scared to go into the vet. She was not scared of people because she was exposed to our friends/family going in and out of our house all of the time. Everyone would pay attention to her. To this day we are still working on her socialization issues. She is getting better, but you will still see her jump once in awhile when she is scared.

I found a puppy Socialization checklist that I would like to share with you. Please view
 this website and print it out to help guide you: https://ultimatepuppy.com/socialization/puppy-socialization-checklist/

You have a lot of responsibilities to tackle with a new puppy. Make sure that this is at the top of your list! Socialization is a never ending process, but it is important to start when your puppy is young. The key is to make sure that your puppy is happy, safe, comfortable, confident as they are discovering the world around them!

6

Conclusion

There you have it! I hope my book was informative and answered every question that you had when thinking of getting a Golden Retriever puppy. I hope you enjoyed reading it as much as I had fun writing it. Enjoy your new Golden! You will be so happy you made the decision to get one!

If you found this book helpful, please leave a favorable review for my book on Amazon! I would greatly appreciate this!

7

Resources

Flaim, D. (2021, April 15). *Signs of a Responsible Breeder*. American Kennel Club. Retrieved from https://www.akc.org/expert-advice/dog-breeding/signs-of-a-responsible-breeder/

Kriss, R. (2016, August 9). *9 Questions to Ask Your Potential Breeder*. American Kennel Club. Retrieved from https://www.akc.org/expert-advice/nutrition/questions-to-ask-your-potential-breeder/

Jake. (n.d.). *How To Pick A Golden Retriever Puppy From The Litter (6 Helpful Tips)*. Golden Hearts. Retrieved from https://goldenhearts.co/how-to-pick-golden-retriever-puppy/

Jake. (n.d.). *How To Potty Train Your Golden Retriever Puppy (In Just 2 Weeks)*. Golden Hearts. Retrieved from https://goldenhearts.co/potty-train-golden-retriever-puppy/

Meyers, H. (2019, August 9). *Puppy-Proofing Tips for Your Home And Yard*. American Kennel Club. Retrieved from https://www.akc.org/expert-advice/puppy-information/puppy-proofing-tips-for-your-home-

and-yard/

Mattinson, P. (2020, November 16). *Puppy-Proofing Tips for Your Home And Yard*. Happy Puppy Site. Retrieved from https://thehappypuppysite.com/golden-retriever-puppy/

Sapra, H. (2021, October 28). *What are the Benefits of Dog Toys? RSS*. Pet Life. Retrieved from https://shop.petlife.com/blogs/news/what-are-the-benefits-of-dog-toys

Printed in Great Britain
by Amazon